CONGENITAL PIPE DREAMS

Poems by Victor Clevenger

Kansas City   Spartan Press   Missouri

Spartan Press
Kansas City, Missouri
spartanpresskc.com

Copyright (c) Victor Clevenger 2017
First Edition 1 3 5 7 9 10 8 6 4 2
ISBN: 978-1-946642-05-9
LCCN: 2017930858

Design, edits and layout: Jason Ryberg
Author photo: Victor Clevenger
Cover photo: Jon Bidwell
All rights reserved. No part of this publication may be reproduced or transmitted in any form or by any means, electronic or mechanical, including photocopying, recording or by info retrieval system, without prior written permission from the author.

ACKNOWLEDGMENTS

Prospero's Books and Spartan Press would like to thank
Jeanette Powers, j.d.tulloch, Jason Preu, M. Scott
Douglass, Shawn Pavey, Shaun Savings, Jesse Kates,
Jim Holroyd, Steven H.Bridgens, Thomas Mason,
Beth Dille, Mason Wolf, Katherine Samet, The West Plaza
Tomato Co. and The Robert J. Deuser Foundation
For Libertarian Studies.

Some of these poems have appeared online at the
following places:

*DeadSnakes.com, Yellow Chair Review, Zombie Logic
Review, & Least Bittern Books.*

Many thanks to the fine editors.

You can contact the author at: www.victorclevenger.com

CONTENTS

trigger etiquette / 1

after a long fight-night / 2

the guillotine experts / 4

last night / 5

i've got some real problems / 6

second hand / 7

gillham park girl / 8

barn wood desires / 9

james / 10

why i preferred bastard friends / 11

whistling, pretty paper / 12

what do you mean / 13

pissing on sidewalks again / 15

through your eyes / 16

ashes, but okay / 18

$3.89 plus tax / 20

the night owl growl with crissy / 22

silly girl / 23

congenital pipe dream / 24

in plainfield, indiana / 25

excellence / 26

road 705 haiku / 27

untouched / 28

buttsex in sunbury, ohio / 29

chicken hungry / 31

porno daydreams / 32

do you remember / 33

meth mistress: poem #1 / 34

meth mistress: poem #2 / 35

meth mistress: poem #3 / 36

meth mistress: poem #4 / 37

meth mistress: poem #5 / 38

meth mistress: poem #6 / 39

meth mistress: poem #7 / 40

meth mistress: poem #8 / 41

the day before my 35th birthday / 42

& i always assume / 43

short stuff: the freedom of my penis / 44

the problem / 46

i stay naked with / 47

porcelain poem / 48

six-one / 49

darkness & solitude / 51

please know / 52

half dead & half alive / 53

you on top, top of me / 56

my words / 57

when you raise / 58

after a little bit you learn / 59

i'm writing / 61

for Crissy Michelle

trigger etiquette

if i am going
to take a
bullet,

then so be it,

but please
make sure

that the
son-of-a-bitch

is at least
meant
for me.

after a long fight-night

the mid-summer moisture falls freely
from the morning sky like soft-rotten
peach pits—rotten fruit in full form
disgusts me.

the blackbirds that sit on all the stoplights
& street signs wait like whores for
chewy vittles, as the moisture slips
preened feather tips.

& i just walked seventeen minutes to a
brand new liquor store out of curiosity
& rich rumors of cheap prices, but the door
is locked at ten o'clock.   w-t-f?

the blackbirds now snicker & whistle that
the drunks wait like whores too—clever
little fucks. i love them.   blackbirds.

they sit high on wires,
they freely shit all over this world,
& it's not the idea of freely shitting all over
something that i love them for.

(although i have my moments where all i
see is a three-ring bullseye, right between the
ignorant eyes of the world)

i love them. blackbirds, because they
seduce me with an any given moment
up & go freedom that aches my
responsibility-grounded bones.   blackbirds.

& i tell you my honest desire, darling,
throughout this love me one day,
hate me the next day relationship that we
nurture—if blackbirds could open beer bottles,
then i would seriously desire wings.

i would fly away with my alcoholism
& your whispers for me to *go away,
no come back, please stay forever,*

would never enter my skyward ears again.

the guillotine experts

all say that

*the act happens so fast that you'd
never feel a thing,*

but how the hell
do they know
that,

they all still have
their heads.

last night

crissy & i ate beef-n-bean burritos
with jalapeno cheese smeared on top,
chicken rice tortilla soup on the
side as we sat at the kitchen table
listening to catfish read a poem about
the statue of liberty's ass on fairfax
radio.

when he finished reading, the other
participants were speechless, crissy
was speechless, & i nodded my head
in solidarity, but in the back of my mind
i wondered if i had lit the candle that
sat in the center of the table, would it
have been romantic enough for her to
consider giving me a jerkjob in the shower
with the V05 shampoo.

i've got some real problems

i've got heroes,
& they got problems
too . . .

knowing this
makes me feel a little
bit better.

second hand

to the young woman
wearing the black
& white bandana,

stocking the racks
at plato's closet,

there are definitely
a hundred thousand
men

who would gladly
fuck you.

gillham park girl

you are a
beautiful dove
beginning to
grizzle from
these dirty
streets
surrounded
by ravens.

i fear
that you will
soon
forget
how to fly
back home
altogether.

barn wood desires

when i was a little boy my nose was
large. it was the size of a full grown
man's nose & i hated my aunt's pig
farm. one day while working the shovel,
i found a secret stash of magazines that
were hidden under the dirty, dead-n-
golden grass in the top loft of the barn.

every morning after breakfast i would run
& climb the rotten peg-steps of the ladder
all the way to the top & thumb through the
pages. i had never seen the inside of a
woman's vagina before, & i had no clue that
a picture could do what it did to my body,
but before the end of that summer, i could sit
up in that loft for hours with a hard-on &
never even smell the shit in the air from the
fresh piles on the ground.

one night lightning struck the loft & it
all ended.

james

an old neighbor told me about
the coffee that he had swallowed
on the navy ships back in the 1960's.

it gets cooked twice, he said, *twelve
hours before you would swallow it,
& it tasted like mud. it looked like a
handful of liquid dirt that had been
swept up from the deck. your insides
would itch & your guts would rage.*

from that point on, i assumed that this
is how my grandfather felt most
mornings, sitting in san diego,

itching & raging as he pulled his white
pants up to his waist.

i could be wrong though,

hell, he might have never even swallowed
the coffee, i'm just assuming that he did.

i don't know, i have never met the guy.

why i preferred bastard friends

i was the type of little squirt who exclusively
enjoyed my own pillow with baseballs on
the case, blankets with tigers creeping
through trees, that worn down mattress that
sunk deep in the middle, & the four walls
that surrounded it all,

so i was out-of-my comfort zone when i
spent the night, for the first time, with him,
but the evening eased along decently as we
ate cheese pizza, watched hulk hogan body
slam andre at mania 3, built a fort with
bedsheets tied to the knobs of his dresser
drawers, & fell asleep before his older
brother came home at curfew & stumbled
across the bedroom floor.

in the morning we woke up early, lifted his
bedroom window which was on the second
floor, spotted a small brown bird, & wasted
it with his slingshot & a red marble; feathers
flew everywhere as we ran quickly down the
stairs to tell the story to anyone, but his
angry father stopped us halfway through the
story & began smacking his hands against
the back of our heads for being what he
called *stupid lil' sonz-uh-bitches* & we
cowered upstairs in the fort until my mother
got there at noon.

whistling, pretty paper

most all of this broken neighborhood
waits for the drop—government checks
into mailboxes.

the mailman gets a good contact high;
he walks around puddles of piss in summer
winds while whistling willie nelson tunes.

one day, he broke his leg, retired, & now
he waits for the drop too.

what do you mean

*she left her husband for
a black man who lives in the city,*

is what the locals used to say,
& usually it was followed with,

*i feel horrible for her children,
& the city is such a goddamn
scary place,*

but i thought, *to hell with those
asshole bastards anyway,* because
i liked the cultural change from
cowboys & cattle farms to working
saturdays at four o'clock in the
morning with her boyfriend on the
docks at defeo produce.

we would pull & pick the primo
tomatoes to be placed on pale
green styro trays & when that
was done,

he would leave to go work at the
city market & i would leave to go
to the apartment with a little bit of
cash in my pocket.

one saturday, i didn't stop at the
apartment on kenwood, i kept
walking up 39th street until i came
to the intersection at troost ave.

i turned left & walked to wicks
tropical fish where i bought the
last red bellied piranha in the tank.

i had always wanted a savage
friend, & now i had one.

while walking back towards the
apartment, i passed a car wash
that was empty, so i walked the
stalls & searched the machines
for loose change;

i found a $1.25 & a pair of brass
knucks.

i held the clear plastic bag high into
the air, & the fish smiled at me
savagely exposing all of his teeth.

i smiled back, & then said to him,
you sure are one pretty motherfucker, amigo!

pissing on sidewalks again

words are my
young mistress
without flesh.

we share minds

we share heart

we share soul

we share agony

we share lack
of consummation

we share
drunken disturbances

we share bars
between us

we share
smiles,

in photos with rotten teeth.

through your eyes

like ice cubes.
through your eyes like marbles.
through your eyes like the knob
on an oil lamp.

give me confessions from anne,
from sylvia.   cold war kids.
give me buk.   give me the beats.
give me the new to me:
selected poems
six sets, 1951-1983:
howard hart

give me the always open door,
the always open hole;
give me the
oh, baby, you're the greatest i have
ever fucked
lie, because i like it….

like suicide notes without signatures,
my early rejection letters:

five2one	third wednesday
perpetual	gargoyle
lotus-eater	brightly press
cactus heart	word riot

give me cheap wine.
give me fat stomachs & smooth
legs.   give me smoky cunt portraits
in #2 lead & remember

i can draw for hours, when you
use your fingers
on yourself,

consider it,

& know there is no elitism in
choosing
to do so,

the same as there is no failure in
choosing not
to do so,

it is just an option,   a suggestion,

& anyways, i just wanted you to know
there were three-dollar scarfs
for sale at the street fair today,

& i bought one for you.

ashes, but okay

never
hesitate
to be the
one who
starts
the fire,
& then
stands
in the
center
of it;
make
this god-
damn
world
rush to
you, &
if nobody
ever
comes then
just
burn
alone,
&
write
poetry

from the
sweet little
smoked-
out spot
behind
your
charcoal
eyes
just like
the rest of
us burnt-
up-beautiful
fuckers
do.

$3.89 plus tax

i sat down on the shithole
in the back of the supermarket, grunted, &
gave it a good run.

my pants dropped down & covered the tops
of my shoes, & through the crack
in the door, i could see three young punks.

aisle boys & grocery bag boys.

one had large holes in the lobes of his ears
& he said, *hurry up, old man, it's my lunch break.*

& i didn't answer him, i just gave another
good run as i held my limp pecker between
my legs, wondering if it would be a good fit
in the punk's earlobe

& one of the other punks, who had zits
(in all stages of growth) on his cheeks said,
jennifer got some good xtc this time from her dealer.

i wiped my ass four times & stood up.

you fucking stink, like my grandpa does,
said one of the kids who had a nose as large as mine.

it was a beautiful goddamn nose & i
winked at him as i walked to the sink to
wash my hands.

i finished & dried them off with paper.

i walked out of the door.

i pulled my phone out of my pocket &
typed this on a notepad app,

then i bought spaghetti for tomorrow—
sardines for today.

the night owl growl with crissy

i will still be writing poetry
at 2 o'clock while she sleeps,
& by 3 o'clock, i will be beside her
in the bed—my body's weight
cutting ruts in the mattress & my
flash bang snores waking her.

she will sit up & contemplate
carrying out my execution,
while repeating the phrase,
shut the fuck up, through clenched
teeth.

my stay of execution will be granted
around 4 o'clock when she finally
falls back to sleep.

her alarms will ring repeatedly at
5 o'clock & she will tell me later in
the day that she slept right through
them, but by 6 o'clock, she will tell me,
that she was up, dressed, & laughing
at the neighbor's cat licking its own
asshole on the hood of that '84 buick
skylark again.

silly girl

you forget that
i know you better
than anyone;

you forget that
between the blowjobs
& the wine
& the weed

i wrote poems
with you

i wrote poems
for you

we wrote the verbs
& nouns
& adjectives
right out of
our souls

until nothing was left

& that feeling of nothing
felt right

that feeling of nothing felt amazing.

congenital pipe dream

a man's cock leaks equally vital ingredients & we
know that within a woman's womb is the new
generation & the possibility of a future that may not
require the need to constantly hope-n-pray
for an existence that contains peace.

in plainfield, indiana

the pumpkin spice pancakes
at the cracker barrel could
have been cooked directly
off of the fleshy ass of the
hispanic woman in the blue
dress, who stood in line
waiting to be seated too.

i guarantee you, at that very
moment, that the griddles in
the kitchen weren't half as
hot as that thing was.

excellence
(for janne karlsson)

brilliant bastards
like you aren't
born everyday.

you are 5 aces
in a sealed card deck
of 52

& you haven't
drawn a set of
tits yet

that i wouldn't
gladly chew
on

when this mad
fucking
world,

as we
know
it,

explodes.

road 705 haiku

where the fuck are we
hat on head like heisenberg
strange dogs say, *hello*

untouched

bombs
are beautiful,

so are
butterflies,

but the
problem is that

heartless
motherfuckers

just have to
touch them
both.

buttsex in sunbury, ohio

we drove the white four-door sedan
six hundred & twenty-four miles,

through four states & who the fuck
knows how many counties until it was almost dark.

we collectively decided that we would
keep left at the fork in the road to continue
on exit 5b, following signs for i-71
n/cleveland until we found sunbury, ohio

& that is where we would shack down.

when we arrived in sunbury, i rented a
room at america's best value inn and suites,
then we unloaded the car—across the street
was a bob evans restaurant.

we walked over for fried chicken, eggs over
easy, hash browns, pancakes, mashed
potatoes, & fresh rolls.

after we ate, paid the bill, tipped the
waitress, walked out the front door & back
across the street,

made it inside room 218,

stripped all of our clothes off, pulled down
the bedsheets, climbed up on the mattress,
& rubbed on each other's bare skin, while
moaning without having to worry about
waking the children, i said to crissy,

*baby, i'm gonna try to stick it in the
backdoor real gently, like i did the last time
we made hotel love, six years ago.*

she said, *um, no you're not.*

& the feeling of nostalgia hung itself from
the rod, next to the shower curtain.

chicken hungry

the lightness
in my beard
at all lengths
is the same color
as this freshly fried
piece of perfection.

porno daydreams

when my mind
goes obscene & unzips,
i just let it do what it does,

life seems a little more pleasurable that way.

do you remember

when we were beautiful disasters,
when painted black fingernails could have
been mine or could have been yours?

the bullet.   the butterfly wings.

when the weight of the world weighed no
more than the weight of jesus,

my boa constrictor,

a death machine coiled like silk around our
necks & when he would get nervous, our
skin would turn a tender rose color from the
pressure,

& we would laugh,

because we knew that there was always that
funny feeling right before jesus
dropped us to our knees
on the tennis court,

& we were too alive in the moment
to know   that we were actually dying.

meth mistress: poem #1

self-medication & isolation seem to be
the only course of action to beat back
my stalking demon which purposely
wears clothing short enough & sheer
enough that i can see more than just the
outline of her bare vagina when i pass
her in the hallway. *go away,* i tell her,
i already have a girlfriend. she just
growls & licks her lips. yesterday, i
contemplated nailing the windows shut.

meth mistress: poem #2

i often wonder what it would
feel like to be chewed up &
swallowed by a demon with
a mouth as amazing as hers.
some nights i lie on the floor,
less intoxicated than other nights,
with both legs under the bed,
both arms stretched above my head,
just hoping to know & never
have to wonder again.

meth mistress: poem #3

there was one time in a hotel
bathroom, after sex, that she
turned the water on & stepped
into the shower. i sat down on
the toilet & took a shit. you
would have thought that we had
been married for years.

meth mistress: poem #4

i still don't love you,
but i like you enough
to wait for the feeling(s)
to change.

meth mistress: poem #5

& after our fights, i would kiss her throat
& whisper, *fuck-fuck-fuck*
just wishing that my four-letter words
were as razor sharp as hers were,
& if so, if they were, her
pearl necklaces & infinity scarves
would never fit quite the same again.

meth mistress: poem #6

understand that i still care about you,
i just scream & act stupid so that you
won't have to scream & act stupid alone.

meth mistress: poem #7

she told me that her heart
would always be mine,
so i took what was mine
& left him a heartless bitch.

one that now has a reason
to dress in clothes that look
as if she had died last tuesday.

meth mistress: poem #8

she broke me real good too,
my heart now mumbles
obscenities like, *cunt*
underneath its breath &
between its broken beats.
& i let it, because she was
the one who once told me,
your heart knows best.

the day before my 35th birthday

& the red sea inside of me is bottled in
modesto; it rolls over each morning as the
bottoms of my feet hit the stained cut pile.

god is catching a catnap under the couch
cushions. i peel bananas for three-year-old
children & try to shake her awake.

my lips are substitutes for fingertips in all
of my dreams. the first pot of coffee is
never strong enough; the second pot of
coffee is always stronger, but i'm bored with
coffee by that point. i drink beer.

there is a jewel inside the stomach of my
desire.

wake up, god, they are gonna riot in
ferguson soon, but i'm sure you already
knew that, right?

& a machine gun in my sister's hands may
be my ultimate demise, but things can only
get better from here, i'm never certain
though, just human, & intrigued by the possibilities.

& i always assume

that this world
is keeping secrets
from
me too,

but it doesn't concern
me much.

we have never
been all that close anyway.

short stuff: the freedom of my penis

1. on my right hip

these 3 funny moles
the same color as toad lips
grow somber gray hairs

2. on the couch cushions

bowl of fresh salsa
ate early & passed out late
to bat-shit wild dreams

3. s.w.a.t.

my penis captured
in a dream the police seized
this town's most wanted

4. search party

my penis escaped
broke free in a goddamn rush
left a note: goodbye

5. upon return

my escaped penis
came back home three days later
smells like rosemary

6. a question

i can't answer that
is my penis amazing
i'll ask her

7. in her opinion

at times it's little
pastel purple night crawler
at times it is huge

8. & in my opinion

her words amaze me
imma swallow her one day
lips first: safe keeping

the problem

i have suicide bones (remarkable)
see-through & protruding like the
hypocotyl, broken apart & twisted
tight like white bread ties.

these bones have life & thrash about.
they are tough motherfuckers & any
man who knowingly has suicide bones
like mine will understand just how tough
they are.

you can't hide them with the other
skeletons inside of coat closets, or inside
of the cupboards with teacups like all
the other men who love life do.
you gotta have a plan:

plan "a"

hide all my suicide bones in all of these
wine bottles & in all of these average
words.

if plan "a" fails, plan "b"

leave a note—
        gone to see grandma, & bukowski.

i stay naked with

the blankets covering the windows —

it's dark at noon, it's dark at night,
& it's dark as the sun rises.

i control the whole
goddamn environment inside,
& it gives me the time to:

sleep, to clip my fingernails,
to masturbate, to hope, to dream, to write,
to stare at myself in the mirror,
to scribble pictures on the paper that i fail
to write words on,
to smoke, to read, to drink myself stupid,
to drink myself satisfied

& find that feeling that tells me i am ready
to face this fucked up world again.

. . . . now,
the bosses at my job,
they just call it all another unscheduled absence
on my performance record, but i,
i call it,

motherfucking essential to my survival.

porcelain poem

i don't wake with hot breath
& hard bones like i once did.

i don't wake with women &
watermelon seeds stuck to my
skin anymore either.

i just wake soft & clean now,
but i still end up alone in a
bathtub at times,

rubbing myself in ways that
older age & responsibility will
never be able to diminish.

sometimes i never even turn the
water on, i just climb in & lie
flat on my back with the porcelain
chill against my skin,

& imagine your face.

six-one

my legs stretched vertical for miles last
night in a dream.

i was paralyzed with one foot stuck inside
the ground & the other foot snagged on
something inside the clouds.

a saxophone played charlie parker tunes for
hours, my bones ached deep into them-
selves, my muscles tried not to let anyone
see them twitch, & my scrotum swayed back
& forth like a tossed about windsock.

my cock fell down limp against my leg like
a teenager who had seen it all, knew it all, &
had done it all.

it pouted & complained that it was
35-years-old & bored, & had nothing to do
except hang around.

i asked it, *how was this different than any
other night, or any other dream?*

it didn't have an answer, so i said to it,
*i am the one suffering, stretched out, aching,
& hoping that i wake up before a bird tries to
build a nest in my spread-open asshole.*

it laughed at the visual it claimed to
now have & I don't remember exactly how
the dream ended, but i woke at 4:42 a.m.
with a hot orange soda on the nightstand.

i took one long drink, stopped, & then took
another long one—my cottonmouth
moistened & i took a long piss into the toilet
soon after.

it was the first day of june already.

darkness & solitude

kick me in the teeth,
until my choppers
crumble into dust

& i spit them out
like spilled sugar
onto the nightstand,

just to say, *hello*

to the morning sun-
shine peering through
my windows with

bittersweet
greetings & groans.

please know
(for s.a.griffin)

anything that you describe to me as,
rare as a pigeon tits wrapped in frog fur,
has my attention.

half dead & half alive

i feel like
an aged man
in this body that
is only
halfway
that.

i sit
alone
for hours
pushing a
pencil.

i don't
speak any
other
languages.

i don't
make good
money.

my neighbors
speak
all different
languages
& make good
money.

they have
scented candles
on their
toilet's
tank.

their
shit
doesn't
smell.

my eyes are
failing me
& my
whiskers
are turning
white.

my guts are
drying out
& my
toenails
are
growing
in.

i have:

acne cream,
hemorrhoid pads,
mouthwash,
& an ashtray

sitting on
the toilet's
tank.

the ashtray
overflows
into the
wastebasket.

maybe one day
i will
put
candles
up there,

but for
now my
shit smells.

it's like a
motivational poster:

PERSEVERANCE.

you on top, top of me

just stay focused, crissy, & keep
pressing on,   keep pressing &
pushing & rubbing against me.

the finish line is rewarding
& we are one slip of your
tongue into my mouth
away from one-hot-mess

& afterwards   as we stand
naked in the bathroom,
rubbing hot watered
washcloths up-n-down our
legs,

you can tell me about how
you almost gave up & i will
tell you about how i would have
never allowed you to

& then we can drink hot tea
in bed,   completely satisfied,
until the children wake up
& we once again argue
about whose turn it is this time
to tuck them back in.

my words

have never given
me great fortune,
or fame,

but they have
given me

my sanity.

& i feel that is a fair
trade these days.

when you raise

children,

you
learn
that
the
couch

is a
hungry
monster

that
swallows
everything.

after a little bit you learn

the mornings
come fast
after
closing
the eyes.

it helps
to jump
up right
before you
close 'em,

rub yourself
clean with
hot water,
cold water
& dry rags.

you smoke
cigarettes &
watch 2 a.m.
television,
call the job to
tell them it's
the shits—

*bad pasta from
the italian joint
over on
cleveland street,*

pour a shot
of gin & a
glass of port,

be a gentleman
& let her
talk about
whatever,
while you sit
undressed
with your
balls
touching
the sofa.

it happens
that way
every now
& again;

it satisfies her,

& then we sleep.

i'm writing

all of our
love scenes
in the
beginning,

because
gunshots
make better
movie plots

& i fully
expect
the closing
credits

to scroll
across a
photograph

of a
tombstone
that reads:

*some holes
are opened
with intentions
of never being
closed.*

Victor Clevenger hopes for the more exciting side of death, as he spends his days in a Madhouse and his nights writing poetry. He sleeps with his second ex-wife and raises his six children in a small town northeast of Kansas City, MO. Selected pieces of his work have appeared at, or are soon forthcoming in, *Poems-For-All, Chiron Review, GTK Journal, Yellow Chair Review, Rat's Ass Review, Blink Ink, Thirteen Myna Birds, the 2016 Hessler Street Fair Poetry Anthology* (Crisis Chronicles Press), *Delirious: A Poetic Celebration of Prince* (NightBallet Press, 2016), *Prompts!* (39 West Press, 2016). Victor's poetry collections include *Come Here* (Least Bittern Books, 2016), and *The More Exciting Side Of Death* (Epic Rites Press/Tree Killer Ink, 2016).

The cover photos for this series were contributed by Jon Bidwell, a photographer who lives and works in Kansas. To view more of his work, visit him at www.instagram.com/jonbidwell.

This project was made possible, in part, by generous support from the Osage Arts Community.

Osage Arts Community provides temporary time, space and support for the creation of new artistic works in a retreat format, serving creative people of all kinds — visual artists, composers, poets, fiction and nonfiction writers. Located on a 152-acre farm in an isolated rural mountainside setting in Central Missouri and bordered by ¾ of a mile of the Gasconade River, OAC provides residencies to those working alone, as well as welcoming collaborative teams, offering living space and workspace in a country environment to emerging and mid-career artists. For more information, visit them at osageac.org

www.ingramcontent.com/pod-product-compliance
Lightning Source LLC
Chambersburg PA
CBHW021450080526
44588CB00009B/780